The Roman Empire

CHRIS HODGSON

Hodder & Stoughton

A MEMBER OF THE HODDER HEADLINE GROUP

Acknowledgements

The Front cover shows a mosaic from the Villa Romana del Casale courtesy of Scala and a cameo of Emperor Augustus courtesy of the British Museum.

The publishers would like to thank the following individuals, institutions and companies for permission to reproduce copyright illustrations in this book:
Araldo de Luca/CORBIS pages 5 (top), 15 (top right), 18 (bottom right), 41; The British Museum-Department of Coins and Medals page 5 (bottom), Arte & Immagini srt/CORBIS page 9 (centre), Archivo Iconografico, S.A/CORBIS page 9 (top left and bottom), 28 (bottom), 29 (bottom), 37 (top left), Farrell Grehan/CORBIS page 9 (top right), C.M. Dixon pages13, 16 (top) (centre right) (left), 17 (top left), 19 (right), 20 (right), 31, 34 (right), 36, 37 (bottom); John Heseltine/CORBIS page 14 (top left), Bettman/CORBIS page 14 (bottom right), 15 (centre right), 29 (top), Dennis Marsico/CORBIS page 14 (centre left), Paul Bigot/University of Caen, MRSH page 15 (top left-scale model of Rome); Archivo Alinari-Firenze pages 14 (bottom left), 15 (bottom right), 37 (centre left); Baldwin H. Ward & Kathryn C. Ward/CORBIS pages 14-15 (main centre picture), 22 (bottom left); Museo della Civilla-Romana/Scala page 16 (bottom right), Mimmo Jodice/CORBIS pages 17 (right), 19 (left) (centre); Fishbourne Roman Palace, Sussex page 18 (bottom left); Infoterra Ltd page 21 (top right); The Ronald Grant Archive pages 22 (top) (bottom right), 32 (all 3); Museo Nazionale-Napoli/Scala page 22 (centre left); Roger Wood/CORBIS page 22 (centre right), 28 (centre left); CADW page 23 (bottom left); Ordnance Survey mapping on behalf of The Controller of Her Majesty's Stationary Office „Crown Copyright MC 100015509 page 24 (right); Science Photo Library page 25 (top); Gianni Dagli Orti/CORBIS page 27 (top); Vanni Archive/CORBIS page 27 (right); BBC page 28 (top); Ruggero Vanni/CORBIS page 29 (centre); Musei Capitolini-Roma/Scala page 37 (centre left); University of Newcastle page 38.

The publishers would also like to thank the following for permission to reproduce material in this book:
David Higham Associates for the extract from Life and Leisure in Ancient Rome by JPVD Balsdon, Bodley Head, 1969; Römisches Freilichtnuseum-Hechingen-Stein for extract from the website www.villa-rustica.de; extracts from New Light Bible reproduced by permission of Hodder and Stoughton, 1998; Chrysalis Books for the extracts from Place Names of Roman Britain by A. Rivet and C. Smith, Batsford, 1979; Lion Publishing for the extracts from The History of Christianity A Lion Handbook, 1990; Professor Margaret Mimber for extracts from http://abacus.bates.edu/~mimber/Rciv/ house.htm; The Penguin Group for the extract from Ancient Rome by Simon James, Dorling Kindersley Ltd, 1997.

Orders: please contact Bookpoint Ltd, 130 Milton Park, Abingdon, Oxon OX14 4SB.
Telephone: (44) 01235 827720, Fax: (44) 01235 400454. Lines are open from 9.00 – 6.00,
Monday to Saturday, with a 24 hour message answering service. Email address:
www.hodderheadline.co.uk

British Library Cataloguing in Publication Data
A catalogue record for this title is available from The British Library

ISBN 0 340 84685 2

First published 2002
Impression number   10 9 8 7 6 5 4 3 2 1
Year   2008 2007 2006 2005 2004 2003 2002

Copyright © 2002 Chris Hodgson

Typeset by Liz Rowe.
Printed in Italy for Hodder & Stoughton Educational, a division of
Hodder Headline Plc, 338 Euston Road, London NW1 3BH.

Contents

THIS CHAPTER ASKS

Why study the Roman Empire?
How did the Romans explain their own origins?

One of the greatest **Empires** of the past was the Roman Empire. Looking at it will help us practise many of the **skills** of being an historian:

■ Seeing that events happen for different reasons.
■ Using evidence like detectives and making decisions.
■ Recognising that historians have different opinions about the past. Deciding why this is the case.
■ Deciding how life in periods of the past is different, or similar, to other periods of history.
■ Using dates and special describing words.

NEW WORDS

EMPIRE: when one group of people defeat and take over the lands of other people. These are then ruled as 'colonies', or 'provinces' of that Empire.
SKILLS: special ways of doing things in order to learn something, or make something happen.

27 BC–AD 14 Emperor Augustus (see pages 27 and 28).

73–71 BC Spartacus revolted against the Romans (see pages 32–33).

44 BC Julius Caesar was killed (see pages 34–35).

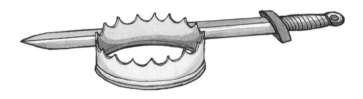

509 BC The Romans got rid of their kings (see page 26).

264–146 BC Wars with Carthage (see page 6).

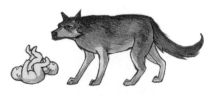

753 BC Romulus and Remus (see pages 4–5).

AD 313 Emperor Constantine became a Christian (see page 40).

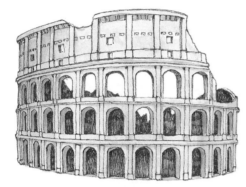

AD 476 End of the Roman Empire (see pages 42–43).

5 BC–AD 33 Jesus Christ (see page 40).

AD 43 Emperor Claudius came to Britain (see pages 10–11).

The centre of the Roman Empire was the city of Rome in Italy. But it was not always a great city. The first Romans were just farmers living on the Palatine Hill, in what would one day be the city of Rome, in about 750 BC. Over the next 500 years this settlement grew into a city and the Romans brought the whole of Italy under their control. After this their power spread around the Mediterranean Sea and eventually much of Europe, North Africa and the Middle East was under the control of the Romans. This lasted until AD 476.

During the time of the Roman Empire many important events happened. Wars were fought with other powerful countries and tribes. Rome became an Empire ruled by an Emperor. Jesus was born in the Roman Empire and the Empire eventually became Christian. Here are some of the world-changing events during the Roman Empire.

Q **1.** Historians use the words 'chronological order' to describe putting events in the order in which they happened. Write out the events on these pages in 'chronological order'.

2. Which of these events do you think was the most important? Explain why you think this.

3. Make a spidergram of all the things that you already know about the Romans.

Who were the Romans?

Who are we?

People often like to tell stories about their country which they feel says something about themselves. In Britain stories like King Arthur make it seem that great and wonderful things were done in the past. Stories like Robin Hood seem to say we think it is good to fight bad rulers and look after the poor. It is unlikely these things really happened in the ways the stories say. What matters is the messages these stories carry. We call these stories with a deeper meaning 'myths'. Like all groups of people the Romans had myths. An important one showed how the Romans were different to the other people living in Italy.

Romulus and Remus

The Roman writer Livy (lived 59 BC–AD 17) told the story of how the origins of Rome could be traced back to Aeneas who had escaped from the city of Troy when it was destroyed by the Greeks. He had travelled first to Carthage in North Africa and then to Italy. One of his descendants, Silvia, was raped by Mars, the god of war. Her twin sons - named Romulus and Remus – were thrown into the River Tiber by her uncle, Amulius, who was jealous of any rivals. Amulius had already driven Silvia's father, Numitor, out of his kingdom and killed Silvia's brothers. But the babies were rescued by a she-wolf and later found by a shepherd.

In time they built a city, with Romulus living on a hill later called the Palatine, and Remus living on the Aventine Hill. The two fought over who should rule and give a name to the city. Remus was killed. Romulus named the city Rome. Later, the neighbouring Etruscan people attacked the city. It was saved when a Roman warrior named Horatius defended the bridge across the Tiber while other Romans chopped up the bridge behind him to stop the Etruscans entering Rome.

History or wishful thinking?

Livy did not make up this story. It was one known to many Romans. They believed Romulus had started the city in 753 BC. When Livy wrote, there were reasons why the story of Romulus and Remus was particularly important:

- Rome had just been divided by a **civil war**. It was important that Romans should unite and stop quarrels.
- The new ruler, **Emperor** Augustus, wanted Romans to believe they had a heroic past.
- At the time many people admired Greek ideas. The story of Romulus and Remus said that Roman history could be traced back to the Trojans who had a city as great as any Greek one.

NEW WORDS

EMPEROR: ruler of an Empire.
CIVIL WAR: fought by members of the same country.

SOURCE A

▲ *What the real Romulus might have looked like. Archaeologists have shown that early Etruscan warriors dressed like this.*

There really have been children raised by wolves. Several have been discovered in India and one was found aged about 11 in France in 1801. However, this does not mean the Romulus and Remus story is true. The wolf story may have been created to suggest they were saved by the Roman gods.

SOURCE B

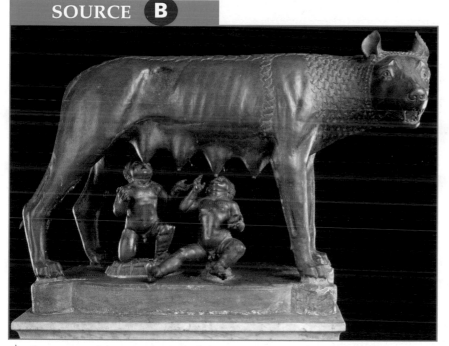

▲ *A statue; but one made by Etruscan craftspeople.*

Is there any truth in the story?

The story is not true. Troy was destroyed in the 12th or 13th century BC. Carthage did not exist until the 9th century BC. Aeneas could not have gone there. And there is no reason to think that Trojans fled to Italy.

But wait a minute! There are some odd clues that suggest there is more to this fairy tale about wolves and babies than first might appear. Archaeologists have found evidence that in about 750 BC two separate villages on the Palatine Hill and Quirinal Hill joined together. This was in the middle of what would one day be the city of Rome. In a part of Rome, later called the Forum, burials have been found dating from the 10th century BC. The early Romans were controlled by a powerful neighbouring people called the Etruscans. They were skilled builders and metal workers. They too had legends about powerful wolves.

1. Imagine you were the ruler Augustus discussing the story of Romulus and Remus with the writer Livy. Explain to him why it would be very useful for Romans to believe in this story at the time when Livy was writing.

2. Look at **Sources B** and **E**. Explain how these show both how important the story was to Romans and how things were perhaps more complicated than the Romans suggested.

SOURCE C

Romulus acted with wisdom given by the gods. He took all the advantages of living by the sea without having any of its disadvantages. He placed his city on the banks of a never failing river whose broad stream flows with a steady current into the sea.

▲ *The Roman writer Cicero writing in about 50 BC.*

SOURCE D

What are you doing? Why are you wasting your time in Africa? If your future fame is not enough, if you will not do it for your own glory, think of your son – the kingdom of Italy and of Rome are his by right.

▲ *The Roman writer Virgil, in about 30 BC, claimed these were the words of the god Mercury to Aeneas in Carthage.*

SOURCE E

▲ *A Roman coin showing the Romulus and Remus myth.*

2 BUILDING AN EMPIRE

THIS CHAPTER ASKS

How did Roman power increase over time?
Why did the Romans want an Empire?
Why were the Romans so successful?

SOURCE A

a. The Romans had conquered Italy by 264 BC. Defending itself against other Italian tribes made Rome the chief city in Italy.

b. The Romans had conquered Spain by 197 BC. They needed to defend land they had won from Carthage.

c. The Romans conquered Greece in 148 BC. Rome had felt threatened by the powerful Macedonians.

g. The Romans conquered Egypt in 31 BC. Removed a threat to Roman power in the eastern Mediterranean.

h. Claudius conquered Britain in AD 43. Brought military victories to an Emperor without any.

i. Trajan conquered Dacia in AD 106. Dacia was a powerful kingdom, Rome had seen it as a threat. Dacia was abandoned in AD 270.

j. The Romans conquered Mesopotamia in AD 115. Rome felt threatened here by the Parthian Empire. Much of this was given up in AD 117.

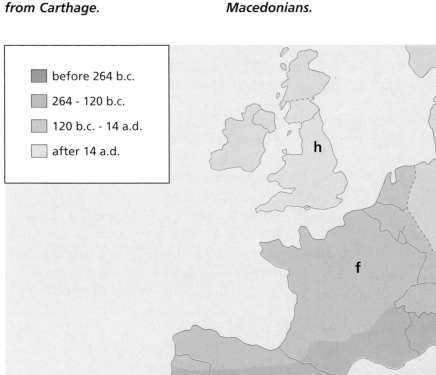

before 264 b.c.

264 - 120 b.c.

120 b.c. - 14 a.d.

after 14 a.d.

Q

1. Create a timeline from 264 BC–AD 115 and place on it the events on these pages. Give it the title: 'Building an Empire'.

2. 'Roman power grew for many reasons'.

Look at your timeline. Choose four events where Roman power increased for different reasons. Explain what these different reasons were and why they led to the Romans ruling more land.

d. After a long war, the Romans conquered Carthage in 146 BC. These wars (the Punic Wars) were fought over trade in the Mediterranean.

e. The Romans conquered the land they called 'Asia' in 133 BC. The last king of Pergamum gave his country to Rome when he died. Rome had earlier helped him against his enemies.

f. In 58–50 BC, Julius Caesar conquered Gaul. Caesar did this to make himself more powerful and ruler of Rome.

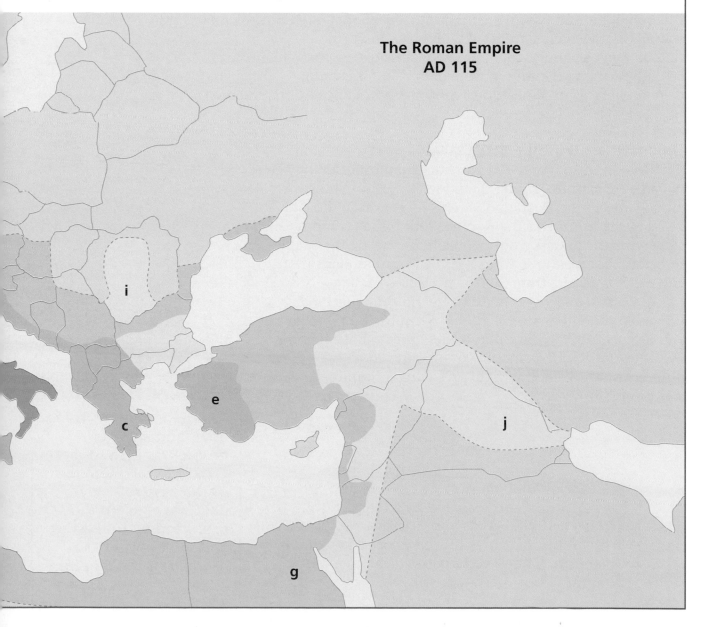

The Roman Empire AD 115

Why was the army important?

The general Domitius Corbulo once had a soldier killed who had put his sword to one side while digging a ditch. A Roman soldier had to be always ready to fight!

THE LEGIONS

During their wars the Roman army became an experienced fighting force. By the 1st century AD there were two main types of soldiers. The first were Legionaries. They had to be **citizens**, were highly trained and joined the army for 25 years. The job provided good pay and a gift of money and land when you retired.

THE AUXILIARIES

Most of the fighting though was done by 'Auxiliaries'. These were not citizens. They were from tribes that had become part of the Empire. Many were cavalry soldiers. When they retired they were made citizens. Both legionaries and auxiliaries were equipped with weapons, armour, shields, swords and spears but legionaries usually had the heaviest armour. Serving in Roman Britain for example were **archers** from Syria and **cavalry** from what is now Hungary and Switzerland!

TRIBES FROM OUTSIDE THE EMPIRE

The Romans also employed warriors from tribes living outside the Empire, giving them the opportunity to earn money and buy Roman goods. This increased in the later years of the Empire as the Romans found they could not raise enough soldiers from people living inside the Empire. In Britain, for example, were boatmen from modern Iraq and other warriors from North Africa and Holland.

The Roman army was an 'Empire building machine'. It needed more than just soldiers. When the Emperor Trajan had a great carving put up in Rome to record his victories over the Dacian tribes in AD 106 this showed all the different skills needed to fight and win an Empire.

A legion was made up of about 5000 men. It was divided up into 'centuries' commanded by a 'centurion'. There were actually 80 men in a 'century' not 100! In the first Roman armies there had been 100 men in a century. Then the structure was changed but the name stuck.

NEW WORDS

ARCHERS: fighters using bows and arrows.
CAVALRY: horse soldiers.
CITIZENS: full members of the Empire. They paid taxes, were protected by the law and took part in the running of the Empire.

▲ *Trajan's column*

Q

1. Look at the evidence from Trajan's column. For each one explain why the skill it shows was needed in the Roman army.

2. Create a commercial to advertise a career in the Roman army.

■ Describe the different kinds of soldiers.

■ Say why it is an attractive career.

■ Explain the different skills needed.

Why did the Romans invade Britain?

It is AD 43. In south-eastern Britain, Roman soldiers are on the march. There are three legions and even war elephants! The Emperor Claudius himself arrives to see the defeat of the south-eastern tribes, stays for just 16 days and then returns to Rome! Soon the legions are on the move again: Legion II Augusta fights along the south coast; Legion IX Hispana advances into the north Midlands; Legion XIV advances into the west Midlands. There will be years of fighting ahead, but large parts of Britain are about to become part of the Roman Empire. But why did this invasion happen?

TRADERS AND INVADERS

Long before the invasion of AD 43 the Romans knew all about Britain. Greek and Roman traders had visited the island, bringing wine from southern Europe and trading it for things produced in Britain. Later, as the Romans conquered Gaul (modern France) they became even more aware of Britain. The tribes in Britain helped those in Gaul who were fighting the Romans.

In 55 and 54 BC Julius Caesar visited Britain. He defeated the British tribes in the south-east of the island. Then he left and returned to Gaul. The British tribes who were most opposed to Rome were forbidden to attack those who were friendly with the Roman Empire. But Britain had *not* been conquered. Those British rulers who hated the Romans had no intention of doing what Romans told them to do!

THE EMPIRE STRIKES BACK

The British tribe of the Catuvellauni (in modern Hertfordshire) crushed the **independence** of the Trinovantes (in modern Essex), who were friends of Rome, in about 30 BC. By AD 40 they were threatening more Roman allies – the Atrebates of modern Berkshire, Hampshire and West Sussex. Verica, king of the Atrebates, fled to Rome to ask for help.

What was Rome to do? A friend of Rome had been defeated. If Rome did not act, then other tribes on the borders of the Empire would no longer value Roman friendship. And there were other reasons too. The new Emperor Claudius wanted a military victory … the British **druids** were encouraging opposition to Rome in Britain and Gaul … there were rumours of great riches in Britain … if enemies of Rome controlled southern Britain a large Roman army would have to be kept in Gaul and this would be expensive and give too much power to possible rivals of the Emperor in command of the army in western Europe. So the Empire struck back!

NEW WORDS

DRUIDS: the priests of the British religion.
INDEPENDENCE: being able to decide yourself how to live your life.

The first Greek traders recorded that Britain was called Prettania. Later Greeks and the Romans changed this to Brettania in Greek and Britannia in Latin. From this comes the name *Britain*.

Main events in the Roman conquest

AD43 Invasion.
AD47 Invasion reaches the river Humber and Wales.
AD60 Invasion of Wales.
AD60 Revolt of Boudicca.
AD74 Northern England conquered.
AD80 Scotland invaded.
AD122 Hadrian's Wall built to keep out fierce northern tribes from Scotland.
AD139 Scotland invaded again. New wall – Antonine Wall – built further north than Hadrian's Wall.
AD164 Roman army withdraws from Scotland. Hadrian's Wall once again becomes the northern border of Roman Britain. Ireland never invaded by Romans.

SOURCE A

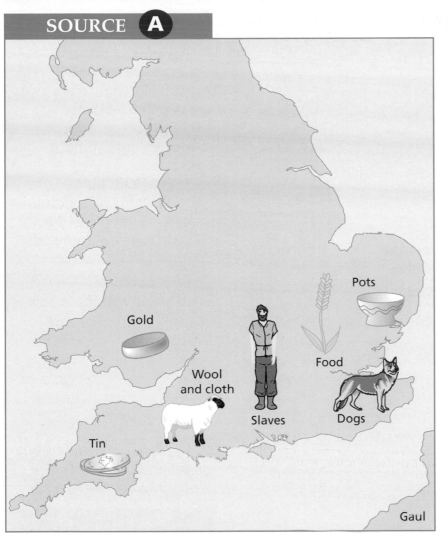

▲ Written by Strabo who lived 64 BC–AD 21. The map shows what the Romans could get from Britain.

SOURCE B

They have simple houses, mostly built with reeds and logs. They are free from the luxury which comes from wealth. They have many kings and rulers. Tin is produced there.

▲ Diodorus Siculus, who lived in about 30 BC.

SOURCE C

The island of Britain is famous in Greek records and our own. Opposite Spain are several islands (British Isles) rich in tin.

▲ Plinius Secundus, who lived AD 23–79.

SOURCE D

The climate is gloomy with much rain and cloud. The soil produces crops and is rich in cattle. The crops are slow to ripen but then spring up quickly. Britain produces gold, silver and other metal. The ocean produces pearls.

▲ Tacitus, who lived AD 56–115.

SOURCE E

There are several islands, rich in tin. Britain has woods and very large rivers and some of them produce gems and pearls.

▲ Pomponius Mela, who lived in AD 40.

Q 1. Look at **Sources A–E**. For each one write down what it suggests as reasons why the Romans might have wanted to invade Britain.

2. From the other evidence in this unit, explain what other reasons Claudius might have had.

3. Write a report to Emperor Claudius giving reasons for invading Britain. Begin it with: 'There are many reasons why we should invade. These include...' End it with: 'I think the most important reason is ...'

Why did Queen Boudicca lose?

YOUR MISSION: To find out why the British failed in their revolt against Rome in AD60

In AD 60 the Romans nearly lost control of their newly conquered land in Britain. Rising in revolt against the Romans British tribes destroyed the new Roman towns at Verulamium (St Albans), Camulodunum (Colchester), Londinium (London). They burnt, crucified and beheaded the people living there. The Britons were led by a woman. She was Boudicca of the Iceni tribe.

WHY REVOLT?

The Iceni tribe lived in modern Norfolk. They were allies of the Romans. When Boudicca's husband, Prasutagus, died he left his kingdom to his two daughters *and* the Roman Emperor Nero. He hoped that way his kingdom would survive as a free ally of Rome. He was wrong. The Romans seized the kingdom. Queen Boudicca was whipped. Her daughters were raped. Iceni chiefs were driven off their land. Not surprisingly the Iceni rose in revolt. With them were their neighbours the Trinovantes of modern Essex.

The Roman **governor**, Suetonius, was far away in North Wales fighting other tribes. There was no one to stop the British wiping out all the Roman settlers in Camulodunum. When the Ninth Legion rushed south it was destroyed. Only its cavalry escaped. Suetonius raced to London, decided it could not be defended, and returned to his army. London and its settlers were destroyed; so was Verulamium. Then Boudicca turned to face Suetonius and his soldiers.

WHY DID THE REVOLT FAIL?

Somewhere on the new Roman road, later called Watling Street, the final battle took place. The Romans had about 7000 Legionaries and 4000 Auxiliaries. Roman writers claim Boudicca had an army of between 100,000 and 250,000. This is probably far too high a guess but she greatly outnumbered the Romans. So, why did she lose after her earlier stunning victories?

NEW WORDS

AMBUSH: a surprise trap.
BARBARIANS: tribes not living like Romans.
GARRISON: group of soldiers defending a fort.
GOVERNOR: leader of the Romans in a Roman province of the Empire.
PLUNDER: stolen goods.

SOURCE A

Those who were unfit for war because of their sex and age, or were too fond of the place to leave, were butchered by the enemy.

▲ *The Roman writer Tacitus on who was in Londinium when Boudicca arrived.*

SOURCE B

The **barbarians** only wanted **plunder**. They passed by fortresses with army **garrisons** and attacked the richest places which were not defended.

▲ *The Roman writer Tacitus.*

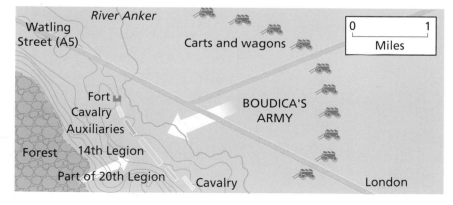

INVESTIGATION

SOURCE C

Win the battle or die. That is what I – a woman –
will do. You men can live on as slaves if that's what
you want.

▲ *Boudicca to her army before the battle, according to the*
Roman historian Tacitus.

SOURCE D

He chose a place approached by a narrow valley
protected from behind by a forest. He made sure no
enemy were behind him. There was no chance of an
ambush.

▲ *Suetonius' plan, according to Tacitus.*

SOURCE E

There are more women than warriors! Most of them
are not trained or equipped for war.

▲ *The Roman governor Suetonius to his army, according to*
Tacitus.

INVESTIGATION

You are the investigator!

Imagine that you are a war journalist travelling with
Roman governor, Suetonius. Write a report to your
newspaper in Rome explaining how and why
Suetonius has succeeded in beating Boudicca.
Remember:

■ Give background information on why the revolt
happened.

■ Describe the early victories of the Britons.

■ Suggest why they were successful at the start.

■ Describe how Suetonius prepared for the final battle.

■ Explain how the two sides were equipped and
trained.

■ Describe how the Romans fought.

■ Explain problems faced by Boudicca's army in
attacking the Romans.

■ Conclude with your thoughts on the main reason
why Boudicca lost the battle.

SOURCE F

The Legions kept their
position, protected by
the narrow valley and
accurately threw their
spears. Then they
advanced in a wedge
shape into the enemy.
The Auxiliaries did the
same. Then the cavalry,
with their lances, broke
through all who resisted.
The enemy fled but
were trapped by their
own waggons which
surrounded them. Our
soldiers killed everyone,
even the women.

▲ *The Roman writer Tacitus.*

SOURCE G

▲ *A tombstone from*
Corinium (Roman Cirencester)
shows a well-armed Roman
soldier killing a poorly armed
British warrior.

3 A CITY AT THE 'CENTRE OF THE WORLD'

THIS CHAPTER ASKS
What was the City of Rome like?
What were the characteristics of a 'Roman way of life'?

NEW WORDS

POLITICS: governing a city or country.

1. The Colosseum. *Opened in AD 80. Gladiators fought here, people were fed to wild animals – all to entertain the Roman crowd.*

3. The Forum. *The original centre of Rome. A market place, centre of law courts, centre of politics.*

7. Aqueducts. *The city of Rome was provided with clean water by these great water channels.*

14

4. Temple of Jupiter. *Jupiter was the chief Roman god. All the people conquered by Rome were expected to worship Jupiter.*

6. Baths. *There were many public baths in Rome; places to meet, talk, have a sauna or a massage.*

5. Pantheon. *Built in 27 BC, it was dedicated to all the gods.*

8. Arch of Titus. *Built in AD 70, it was one of many monuments built to celebrate battles won by Rome.*

2. Circus Maximus. *The site of chariot races. It could seat 250,000 spectators.*

Q **1.** Describe a walk through ancient Rome. 'Visit' the places shown on the modern reconstruction. Imagine a conversation with friends when you return to the Roman Province of Britain again. Describe what you saw and your impression of the capital of the Roman Empire.

Why were cities so important?

Are you interested in politics? Are you civilised? Well, whatever your answer, Romans believed that if you did not live in, or have, a society which had cities you were second rate. The word 'politics' comes from a Greek word meaning city. The word 'civilised' comes from a Latin word meaning city. Why did the Romans (and the Greeks before them) think that cities were such a big deal?

NEW WORDS

AMPHITHEATRE: places where gladiators fought and criminals were executed to entertain.
BASILICA: public building used for trials and government business.

LIVING WHERE THE ACTION IS

For Romans a city summed up everything that they thought went with being really smart, educated, civilised.

- Being well built and well organised.
- Centre of a well-run government with a **basilica** building where local government was discussed.
- A place to carry on trade in a Forum or market.
- Having luxuries like aqueducts, baths, toilets.
- Places where the entertainment was modern and impressive, with theatres and **amphitheatres**.

'WHEN IN ROME ...'

'... do as the Romans do' goes an old saying. But the Romans wanted every people they conquered to live like Romans. Which was why in every place they conquered they encouraged the building of towns and cities. These would show people just how impressive Roman life was.

Julius Caesar hated traffic jams and said that carts could only come into Rome by night. So the streets were safe by day but the noise of traffic stopped people getting to sleep at night!

They would make people glad they were part of the Empire. And they would provide places where taxes could be collected, trade carried out and from which the local area could be governed.

SOURCE A

SOURCE B

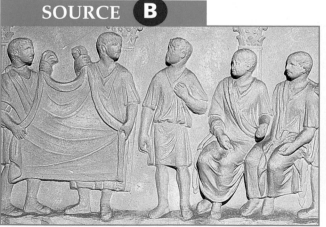

▲ *Roman shops.*

SOURCE C

In places as far apart as North Africa and what is now Northern England towns and cities gave people a little taste of Rome. By the end of the Roman Empire there were about 100 walled 'towns' in Roman Britain. Many of them were very small and unimpressive by Roman standards. In the Eastern parts of the Empire the towns and cities were far more impressive. But even in this province on the edge of the world there were 'little bits of Rome' for the local people to enjoy and be impressed by!

SOURCE D

▲ *Reconstruction based on Source G.*

SOURCE E

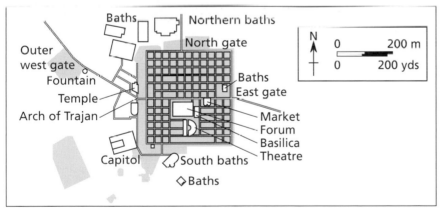

▲ *The new Roman city of Timgad in North Africa had all the planning and facilities Romans expected from 'civilisation'.*

SOURCE F

▲ *A street in Pompeii.*

Q

1. Show that you understand the meaning of the words 'politics' and 'civilised' by writing two sentences, each using one of these words.

2. Look at the Sources in this unit. Explain how each one illustrates the attraction of living in a Roman town.

3. Can you think of any problems of living in a large town which are not referred to here. Think about: health, hygiene, noise, dangers.

4. a. Why did Romans think that city and town life was so important?

b. Why were they keen to build cities and towns in areas which had never seen them before?

A home from home

In what kinds of house did wealthy Romans live in the countryside? And how did poorer people live in the towns?

HOUSE **1**

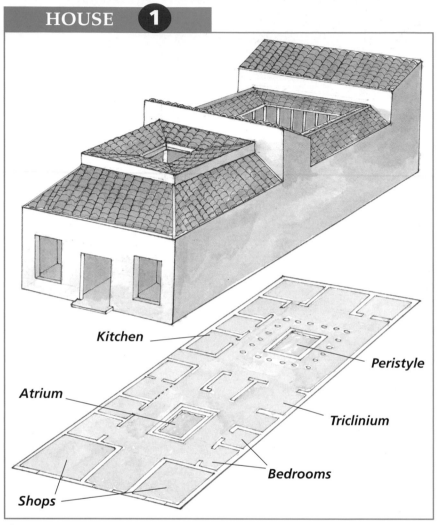

Kitchen

Peristyle

Atrium

Triclinium

Bedrooms

Shops

▲ Plan of a wealthy Roman's house from Pompeii, Italy.

At some very wealthy dinner parties, people were keen to eat so much food that they took something to make themselves sick between courses!

HOUSE **2**

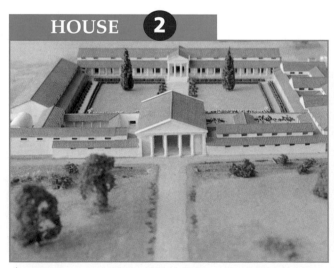

▲ Modern reconstruction of a wealthy country house – Fishbourne Roman Palace in Sussex .

HOUSE **3**

▲ Modern reconstruction of where most people in Rome lived – cheap flats.

SOURCE A

▲ *An atrium discovered by archaeologists in the Roman city of Pompeii.*

SOURCE B

▲ *A peristyle from a house in Pompeii.*

SOURCE C

▲ *Hypocaust system.*

SOURCE D

The garden (peristyle) was ringed by open corridors. Sometimes the peristyle might include a fishpond or swimming pool instead of a garden. It was surrounded by bedrooms and dining rooms. Behind these were servants' rooms and kitchens.

▲ *Modern description of a wealthy Roman's town house.*

SOURCE E

We live in a city kept up by props holding up the tottering houses, with patches covering the cracks in the old walls. Those inside sleep under a roof ready to fall on them. Neighbours shout for water; smoke is pouring out of your third floor attic. But you don't know about it because if the fire-alarm is shouted on the ground floor the last man to know is the one living on the top floor. But all he has is a bed too small for him and a table with a little cup so he hasn't got much to lose!

▲ *Roman writer Juvenal on life in a Roman block of flats.*

SOURCE F

The villa was first built at the end of the 1st century AD and enlarged over 100 years. An open corridor linked the main building with a bath house. At the corners of the villa two 'wings' jutted forward connected by an open air corridor. Behind the house was a large courtyard surrounded by rooms. Some were kitchens and others had underground heating.

▲ *Description of a villa at Hechingen-Stein, south-west Germany.*

Q

1. Match **Houses 1–3** with their correct description Sources **D**, **E**, or **F**.

2. Imagine you are a Roman estate agent. Prepare a description (including pictures) of
- A rich town house.
- A poor flat in a block.
- A wealthy country villa.

3. What kinds of crafts and skills would rich Romans have relied on to keep their home running?

Splash!

WATER, WATER EVERYWHERE …

Today we take clean water for granted. We have it to drink, bathe and shower in, wash our clothes and dishes in. But in many parts of our world people do not have clean water. And for most of history people did not have clean water. And they often died because of this!

WHY WATER?

The Romans did not know about germs but they had already noticed that dirt and disease went together. A Roman military **manual** advised soldiers not to camp near dirty water and not to drink it. Because of this, water was used by the Romans in many different ways:

■ Clean water was brought into Roman towns and cities in channels called aqueducts. The ones supplying Rome carried 1000 million litres of water every day.

■ Public toilets and sewers kept waste out of the supply of drinking water and water was sometimes used to carry away the waste. These were not private places. People sat side-by-side and chatted. Instead of toilet paper there were sponges on sticks, cleaned in pots of vinegar between uses.

■ Keeping clean became a popular leisure activity. Huge public baths became places where people met to swim, relax in different temperatures of water, eat, drink, meet friends. Some were also thought to bring healing such as the baths at the hot spring at Aquae Sulis (Bath, England) where it was believed that the goddess Sulis-Minerva lived in the hot spring. Bathing was so popular that when the Roman army, in the 2nd century AD, investigated why one of its regiments was so badly behaved, it was discovered that its officer spent the day in the baths!

NEW WORDS

BRAWLER: a person causing a fight.
MANUAL: a book saying how to do something.

SOURCE A

When I think of all that water carried such a great distance I say that there has never been anything so amazing in all the history of the world.

▲ *The Roman writer Pliny, who lived AD 23–79.*

SOURCE B

▲ *The aqueduct at Segovia, Spain. It runs ten miles and its tallest arches are 39 metres high. It was built shortly after AD 100.*

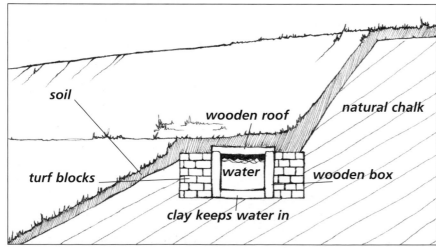

soil
wooden roof
natural chalk
turf blocks
water
wooden box
clay keeps water in

▲ *Diagram of the Aqueduct dug to supply the Roman town of Dorchester, Dorset.*

SOURCE **C**

I live over a bathing establishment. Picture the assortment of noises. When the stronger fellows are exercising and swinging heavy weights I hear their groans. Then there's a lazy fellow content with a rub-down. I hear the slap of the hand massaging his shoulder. Add to this the voice of a **brawler** or a thief, or the chap who likes to sing in the bath and those who jump in with a mighty splash. Imagine the hair plucker keeping up a constant chatter to attract more attention and never silent except when making a customer yell. Then there are the cries of the sausage seller and sellers of cakes and all the peddlars from the cook shops selling their wares, each with their own peculiar voice.

▲ *The Roman writer Seneca, in about AD 63.*

SOURCE **D**

▲ *Remains of the aqueduct of the Roman town of Dorchester, Dorset.*

ROMAN BATHS

◄ *Activities experienced in a visit to the baths.*

Q

1. Describe the different ways the Roman use of water made towns and cities more pleasant to live in.

2. Which do you think was most important?

3. Describe a visit to a public baths. Mention:

■ How water is brought into the town.

■ The stages you go through in the baths.

■ The kinds of people you might meet.

■ Why a trip to the baths was so popular.

Blood sports!

INVESTIGATION

YOUR MISSION: to find out how the Romans entertained themselves with blood sports

NEW WORDS

AMPHITHEATRE: The arena surrounded by seats from where spectators watched.
GLADIATORS: Slaves and prisoners trained to fight to the death.

The fine sand used to soak up blood in the Colosseum was brought from Egypt to Rome. The Latin word 'arena' means 'sand'.

SOURCE A

▲ *A modern reconstruction of a chariot race.*

SOURCE B

▲ *A gladiator's helmet discovered at Pompeii, in Italy.*

SOURCE C

▲ *A mosaic from North Africa showing gladiators fighting wild animals. On the left a criminal is fed to a leopard.*

SOURCE D

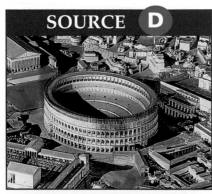

▲ *Model of the Colosseum, Rome, where people fought to the death to entertain the crowd.*

SOURCE E

▲ *A scene from the modern film, 'Gladiator'.*

SOURCE F

If they lose, let them die

All the girls love Celadus the Gladiator

Pugmax won three fights Murranus was killed

▲ *Graffiti such as this was discovered in Pompeii.*

SOURCE G

I demand that this day, from this hour, from this moment that you torture with pain and kill the horses of the Green and White teams. And that you kill and bring into collision the drivers Clarus, Felix, Primulus and Romanus.

▲ *Curse made by a supporter of either the Blue or Red chariot teams in Rome against rival teams.*

SOURCE H

▲ *Amphitheatre from Caerleon, Wales.*

SOURCE I

The Spring Races are on at the moment and all Rome is at the Circus. The Spring Races are perfect for trendy young men! They can place a few bets and sit around posing with their trendy girlfriends!

▲ *Written by the Roman, Juvenal, in about* AD *100.*

SOURCE J

▲ *Stone carving of two gladiators.*

INVESTIGATION

You are the investigator!

You are a modern sports jounalist trying to discover how Roman crowds were entertained by sports which put other people in great danger, or actually involved watching people die.

■ Divide the sources into Primary Sources (from Roman times) and Secondary Sources (from later than Roman times).

■ Decide which sources you think are most useful and any which you think may be less useful. Explain why.

■ Describe the different 'deadly sports' enjoyed by the Romans. Include any details about how they were organised.

■ Explain what you can discover about how Roman people felt about these sports.

■ Decide whether any modern sports can be compared with these Roman sports.

Then write your report with a paragraph on each of these different areas.

Roaming roads!

YOUR MISSION: To build a Roman road.

LOOK AT THE STATE OF THE ROADS

A true story from AD 417. The Roman Empire is in trouble. It's seven years since invading Goth tribesmen have captured Rome itself but Rutilius Namatianus, a rich landowner from the province of Gaul, is more concerned about the state of the roads in Italy. He writes a letter home to a friend in Gaul telling him what a mess the roads are in. No one has repaired the broken bridges. The inns beside the road – where the riders of the Imperial postal service rested and changed their horses – are in ruins.

This is not good enough! This is not what we expect from the Roman Empire!

Look at the notes below and the other information in this Investigation. How should the roads have been built and cared for?

NEW WORDS

GROMA: a wooden pole topped with a cross shape and hanging weights used by engineers to plan the course of a road.

SOURCE A

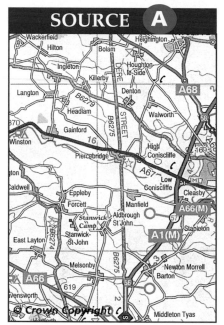

▲ *Modern map showing a Roman road (yellow one) still in use.*

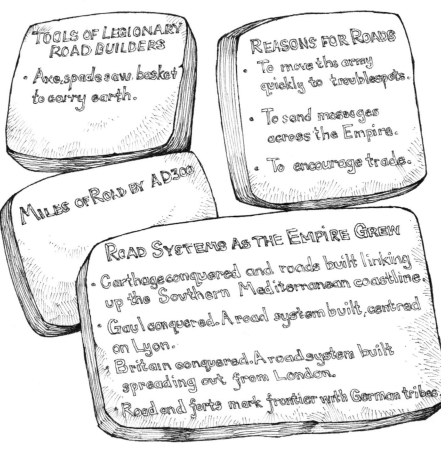

TOOLS OF LEGIONARY ROAD BUILDERS
- Axe, spade, saw, basket to carry earth.

REASONS FOR ROADS
- To move the army quickly to troublespots.
- To send messages across the Empire.
- To encourage trade.

MILES OF ROAD BY AD 300

ROAD SYSTEMS AS THE EMPIRE GREW
- Carthage conquered and roads built linking up the Southern Mediterranean coastline.
- Gaul conquered. A road system built, centred on Lyon.
- Britain conquered. A road system built spreading out from London.
- Road and forts mark frontier with German tribes.

Many of the straight sections of modern British A-roads still follow the course of Roman roads which were built over 1500 years ago. Look at a map of your home area and see if you can find an example.

SOURCE B

▲ *Building a modern road in Britain.*

SOURCE C

The engineer surveys the road with a **groma**. A man marks out the course of the road with stakes. A plough loosens the dirt. It also marks the edge of the road. Workmen dig a trench. The spare earth is carried away in baskets. The earth is beaten flat. Sand is put down. Large stones are put down and cemented together. The next layer is made up of concrete and small stones. Then comes gravel or sand. The road is curved to drain off water. Blocks of stone may finish the surface.

▲ *Description of Roman road building by Vitruvius, who lived from 90–20 BC.*

Clearing trees

Surveyor decides route of road

Pounding top stones together

Pebbles

Curved surface drains off water

Sand and gravel

Big stones

Fixing kerb stones

Layer of concrete and stone

Building a new road in the Roman Empire.

INVESTIGATION

You are the investigator!

Imagine you are Rutilius writing your letter to a friend in Gaul. Explain why roads are so important. Describe how they spread as the Empire grew. Describe how they were built. Conclude by identifying problems which a collapse of the road system will cause.

4 POWER AND POLITICS

THIS CHAPTER ASKS

How was Rome ruled?

How did this change over time?

How was this challenged?

NEW WORDS

REPUBLIC: government without a king or queen.

A BRIDGE TOO FAR …

The Roman historian, Livy, recorded one of the most famous stories of ancient Rome. The Etruscan king Tarquin the Proud aided by Lars Porsenna, Etruscan king of the city of Clusium, attacked Rome. They knew what an important place it was with its bridge over the River Tiber. They caught the Romans by surprise and for a moment it looked as if they would cross the bridge and capture the city.

But they were stopped by one Roman warrior, Horatius, and his two friends. Together they fought off the advancing Etruscans while other Romans cut down the bridge behind them. At last the bridge collapsed. Horatius leapt into the river and swam back to his friends. Rome was saved.

FROM KINGS TO REPUBLIC

What is all this about? Why was this story so important to later Romans? The answer is that, like the legend of Romulus and Remus, it reminded Romans of a very important part of their history. It was a time when Rome stopped being run by kings – and foreign kings at that, which made it worse from a Roman point of view – and became a **republic**.

The first Romans were under the control of a neighbouring people, the Etruscans. According to later Roman legends, Etruscan kings ruled Rome from 616 BC to 510 BC. In this last year the Romans threw out Tarquin the Proud, the last king. Rome became a republic. Tarquin tried to recapture Rome but failed – that's why the story of Horatius was so important to later Romans.

RUNNING THE REPUBLIC

Without a king the running of Rome was in the hands of the *Senate*. These were the leading wealthy citizens of Rome (the *patricians*). Patrician families were very powerful. They often led a group of less powerful people who relied on them for jobs and help. These were their *clients*. Powerful patrician families would compete with each other for control of Rome. The senate often met in, or near, the *Forum*. This was the centre of Rome, with markets, temples, shops and law courts. Each year the senate elected two *consuls* to run the government of the city.

LIFE AT THE BOTTOM

Most Romans were not patricians. Most were poorer and tried to become the clients of patricians in order to get on in life. The poorest Romans were called *plebeians*, or *plebs*. In time the plebs forced the patricians to agree to a set of laws – the Twelve Tables – which gave the plebs more rights and their own representative to defend them. These were called *tribunes*. In the 4th century BC plebs were given the right to stand for election to be a consul and share in power.

At the very bottom of society were *slaves*. These were not citizens, had no rights and could be bought and sold. They did most of the hard work in Rome. They were often captured in foreign wars.

SOURCE A

In the last century BC a series of generals built up military and political power, pushing the Republic towards dictatorship. The first over-mighty general was Marius.

▲ *C. Scarre,* **Penguin Historical Atlas of Ancient Rome,** *1995.*

SOURCE B

▲ *A reconstruction of senators in their* togas – *the long white robe which marked a person as a Roman citizen.*

NEW WORDS

BARBARIANS: tribes living outside Roman control and the Roman way of life.
HEIR: a person who inherits the wealth (and sometimes the power) of another person.

SOURCE C

He knew Romans hated kings. He proclaimed the restoration of the old Republic, with himself simply as first citizen.

▲ *An historian's comment on Augustus' skills, 1990.*

FROM REPUBLIC TO EMPIRE

From 510 BC to 27 BC Rome was a republic. But things began to change. Around 130 BC the Gracchus brothers – both rich Romans – tried to win support by sharing out land to poorer Romans. They were murdered by other rich senators.

In 101 BC the general, Marius, defeated **barbarian** tribes invading Italy and allowed poor Romans into the army. After this other generals tried to increase their power with the support of poorer Romans in their armies.

In 82 BC General Sulla succeeded in making himself a dictator, which meant he ruled like a king. The republic was in deep trouble.

In 62 BC another general, Pompey, and two younger politicians, named Crassus and Julius Caesar joined together to run Rome between themselves. Eventually, in 44 BC, Caesar – who had made himself supreme ruler – was murdered by senators trying to protect the republic. In 27 BC, after a civil war, Caesar's **heir**, Octavian made himself Emperor. He took the new name of Augustus. The republic was over. The Empire had begun.

Q

1. Using the words 'king', 'republic', 'patricians', 'plebs', 'senate', 'consul', 'tribune', 'dictator' and 'emperor' explain how Roman government changed, 510 BC–27 BC.

SOURCE D

As the years passed, Augustus' power grew. The outward ways of running the Republic, with their popular elections, continued but Augustus said who should be elected.

▲ *J.M. Roberts,* History of the World, *1976.*

SOURCE E

▲ *Statue of Emperor Augustus.*

The Emperors

THE FIRST EMPERORS

After the death of Julius Caesar there were 17 years of war. The eventual winner of these wars, in 27 BC, was a man named Octavian. He made himself the first Emperor of Rome. He ruled from 27 BC to AD 14.

Emperors continued to rule Rome until the collapse of the Empire in the fifth century AD. Five of the most famous Emperors lived between 27 BC and AD 68. We know a lot about them because their lives were described by a Roman writer named Suetonius. Historians call this first group of Emperors the Julio-Claudians. They were all related but none was son of the previous Emperor.

Our summer month of August is named after a Roman month which came from the title 'Augustus' which Octavian took as his name. The month of July comes from the month named after Julius Caesar.

A famous film about Claudius made in 1976 – and based on books by Robert Graves – is 'I, Claudius'. It includes almost everything that Suetonius wrote.

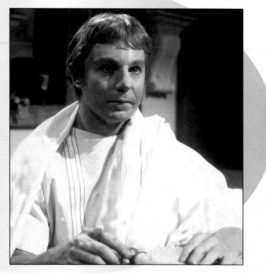

Augustus 27 BC–AD 14.	What Suetonius said	What historians think
	He was a popular ruler. He brought good government and was loved by the Roman people.	He gave Rome a strong and **centralised** government. Trade grew and wealth increased. Writing and the arts increased and Rome was improved by many fine buildings. He killed those who opposed him.
Tiberius AD 14–37	He hated his wife. He forced money out of wealthy Romans and killed those who opposed him. He was hated by the Roman people who welcomed the news of his death.	He followed Augustus' advice and tried not to conquer more territory as Rome could not control it. He was good with money.

Q

1. a. If you were making a modern film about the lives of the first five Emperors, would you be more likely to use the descriptions written by Suetonius or the views of modern historians? Explain your reasons.

b. What does this tell you about how careful you need to be when using films to get an idea about events in the past?

2. Suetonius wrote in AD120, many years after the events he described. What would you need to know in order to decide how reliable he is as an historical source of information?

3. Using the evidence, write an imaginary conversation with Suetonius explaining ways in which modern historians agree/disagree with his opinions.

Caligula AD 37–41	What Suetonius said	What historians think
	He was a mad monster who thought he was a god. He had people killed while he ate his dinner and invited rich Romans to dinner and then took their wives. He murdered anyone he did not like. He slept with his sisters and when one became pregnant he killed and tried to eat the baby.	His wild behaviour angered many powerful Roman senators. He relied for power on his bodyguard – the Praetorian Guard – but they eventually murdered him. Some of the worst stories are probably not true but he did commit terrible crimes.
Claudius AD 41–54	He was crippled. He was not very intelligent. He hid when Caligula was murdered but soldiers found him and made him Emperor. As Emperor he let other people make the important decisions.	During his time as Emperor his friends, close servants and advisors became very powerful. He invaded Britain in AD 43 because he needed the fame of a military victory. He was popular but became more brutal against opposition as time went on.
Nero AD 54–68	He slept with his mother. He tried to turn a boy into a girl and then married him. He set fire to Rome so he could build a new palace called the 'Golden House'. He killed Christians so they would be blamed for the fire. He went out at night and attacked people.	His rule began quite well but when he faced opposition he became very brutal and cruel. He crushed all opposition and lost support of the powerful Senators. He did not start the fire but did kill Christians. There were revolts in Spain and Gaul. He was deserted by his guards and committed suicide.

THINKING IT THROUGH

Think like a Roman ...

How did Romans think? How did Romans view the world? What kind of people were the Romans? It's hard to answer these questions because they were as varied and complicated as people ever are. But if we look carefully at some of the things educated Romans wrote we can get an idea of what these people, at least, thought was important. We can see what they felt being a Roman was all about.

KNOWLEDGE IS POWER ...

Romans valued education. This only applied to boys from rich families. Some were taught at home by educated slaves, who were often Greek. Later they attended schools where they learned a range of subjects, including **oratory**. This prepared them for a life in the government, the law, or as an officer in the army. It helped them run their **estates**. The best poorer children could hope for was to be trained in a job by a craftsman, or to get a rich man as a **patron**, who would pay for their education. Sometimes poorer people put their money together to hire a teacher to teach their sons. They knew that education was the way to get on in the Roman world.

NEW WORDS

ESTATES: land.
ORATOR: a skilled and trained speaker, skilled in **ORATORY**.
PATRON: a rich person who helped a less powerful citizen and was owed loyalty in return.

Roman numbers made it very hard to do maths. For instance, 88 was written as LXXXVIII. Such numbers took up a lot more space than ours do, which are based on Arab numbers not Roman ones.

Our ancestors were not ashamed to copy what was useful from other people. They copied the armour and weapons from the Samnites. Most of their official robes were copied from the Etruscans. In fact they copied any useful idea, whether it came from a friend or an enemy.

Julius Caesar, lived 100–44 BC.

You will need both leisure and intelligence to follow what I have to say. Your mind must be free from all distractions.

Lucretius, lived 94–55 BC.

We paint, make music, even wrestle better because the Greeks have taught us how. In fact, although we conquered Greece, they conquered us.

Horace, lived 65–8 BC.

Augustus filled his house with the huge stone remains of sea- and land-monsters, which people call 'Giants' Bones'.

Suetonius, AD 69–130.

30

SOURCE A

▲ *Arriving late to a Roman school.*

Q It is AD 510 – a century since Britain ceased to be part of the Roman Empire. However, in the West of Britain the parents of Gildas – who will one day become a famous monk and writer – are still determined to try to educate him in the Roman way! The young boy asks them why?

Use the evidence in this unit to give their reply. Mention:

■ What Romans felt about education.

■ How they were keen to learn about the world.

■ How they were not afraid to learn from their neighbours and even from people they had conquered.

■ What kinds of knowledge and skills education would provide.

■ Why education led to power.

People of the Roman Empire valued the education brought by Rome. As late as 100 years after the end of Roman Britain rich familes in Western Britain still tried to give their sons a 'Roman education'.

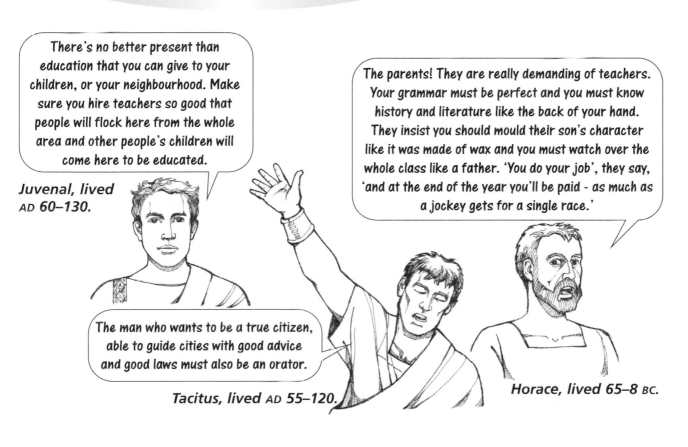

There's no better present than education that you can give to your children, or your neighbourhood. Make sure you hire teachers so good that people will flock here from the whole area and other people's children will come here to be educated.

Juvenal, lived AD 60–130.

The parents! They are really demanding of teachers. Your grammar must be perfect and you must know history and literature like the back of your hand. They insist you should mould their son's character like it was made of wax and you must watch over the whole class like a father. 'You do your job', they say, 'and at the end of the year you'll be paid - as much as a jockey gets for a single race.'

The man who wants to be a true citizen, able to guide cities with good advice and good laws must also be an orator.

Tacitus, lived AD 55–120.

Horace, lived 65–8 BC.

Spartacus

SPARTACUS – THE HOLLYWOOD FILM

First released in 1960 and restored in 1991, *Spartacus* is a classic Hollywood film. In the film Spartacus was a Greek from the conquered province of Thrace. He was sold as a child to work in the mines of Libya in North Africa. While there he is bought by Lentulus Batiatus, the owner of a gladiator training school. While being trained, Spartacus meets a British slave girl named Varinia and they fall in love. A visiting and cruel Roman, Crassus, orders a fight to the death for entertainment and buys Varinia.

Spartacus cannot stand this treatment. He leads a revolt of the gladiators. The revolt succeeds and thousands of slaves flock to join them. Spartacus and his gladiator friends train them and together they fight two great battles against the Romans. The slave army wins both battles.

Finally Crassus leads an army against Spartacus. This time the Romans win. He says he wants Spartacus but the slaves refuse to say who he is and each shouts out, 'I am Spartacus'. Crassus crucifies thousands of slaves. Crassus is in love with Varinia and jealous of Spartacus. He guesses which slave is Spartacus and keeps him, and his best friend, as the last two slaves die.

NEW WORDS

PLUNDER: to rob and steal from other people.

A slave working on a villa estate was expected to live only ten years.

Some slaves were well educated in order to teach the children of the household in which they lived.

Spartacus is made to fight and kill his friend. Then he is crucified. Lentulus is persuaded to rescue Varinia who shows Spartacus their baby before she escapes.

SOURCE A

If we win I will have many and better horses taken from my enemies. If we lose I will not need a horse.

▲ *Spartacus, as he killed his horse before the last battle.*

SOURCE B

He was high spirited, brave, intelligent and gentle.

▲ *Spartacus, described by the Roman writer Plutarch.*

SPARTACUS – THE REAL STORY

The Romans Plutarch and Appian wrote about the slave revolt of 73 BC.

Crassus crucified 6000 slaves along the road leading to Rome.

Spartacus came from Thrace. He seems to have fought in the Roman army. He deserted, was captured and then sold into slavery as punishment. He was bought by Lentulus Batiatus and trained as a gladiator. He had a Greek wife.

Spartacus led a revolt and gathered about 70,000 slaves on Mount Vesuvius. He defeated the Romans in seven great battles and reached the Alps in northern Italy.

Greek slaves were highly prized as teachers, doctors, accountants and artists.

In the film *Spartacus* the final battle scene was filmed in Spain, not in Italy, and employed 8000 extras from the Spanish army.

In 73 BC about a third of the people living in Italy were slaves. This made it easier to carry out great building projects because the lives of the workers were so 'cheap'. Others were bought to replace them.

Spartacus could have escaped from Italy. However, his followers refused to leave; they wanted to plunder Italy and Spartacus ended up leading them back down to Southern Italy again.

At this point the Senate sent Crassus, a leading Roman, to crush the revolt. Spartacus headed north again but the Romans, under Crassus, defeated him. He died in the battle, though his body could not be identified.

Spartacus took 167 days to film and won four Oscar awards.

In the film thousands of slaves cry, 'I am Spartacus'. The noise was actually recorded at an American Football game with the crowd yelling out the words.

Q 1. How historically accurate was the film *Spartacus*? Make a table with two columns. Head one with: 'Things about the film which are accurate' and the other with 'Things about the film which are historically inaccurate'. Then make your final decision on how accurate you think it is.

A Roman murder

YOUR MISSION: to find out why Julius Caesar was murdered.

In 44 BC the powerful Roman politician and general, Julius Caesar, was murdered in the Forum in the centre of Rome. His murder can tell us a lot about:

- How the way Rome was ruled changed in the last years of the Republic.
- Conflicting ideas different Romans had about how Rome should be run.
- Why it was becoming easier for one person to rule Rome.

Look and decide why Caesar was murdered.

INVESTIGATION

ALLY: friend and supporter.
DICTATOR: a person who rules without having to share power.

Caesar was fond of wearing red boots. This worried some Romans because traditionally these boots were worn by kings.

LIFE OF JULIUS CAESAR

100 BC	Born a member of a very rich family.
67 BC	Elected to the Senate.
58 BC	Begins conquest of Gaul.
55 and 54 BC	Invaded Britain but withdrew after a short time here.
49 BC	Invaded Italy and took power in Rome.
48 BC	Defeated Pompey, an **ally** who had turned against him. Invaded Egypt and put a new ruler – Cleopatra – in control.
46 BC	Defeated more rivals in battle. In Rome he brought in laws to help poorer Romans.
44 BC	In February made himself **dictator**. Murdered in March by a group of senators.

When Caesar entered the Senate they stood up as a sign of respect. Each assassin drew his knife. Caesar received 23 wounds. Others watched in horror. They did not dare run away, or help Caesar, or make a sound. Many of the assassins wounded each other as they fought to stab so many knives into his body.

He accepted too many honours. He became consul several times and then dictator for life. He was happy to be treated like a god, with a gold throne, a statue alongside statues of gods, a month of the year named after him. He would not stand up to greet the Senate and they hated him for this. Someone placed a laurel wreath with a white ribbon [a king's badge] on his statue. Caesar told off the officials who removed it. From that time onwards the rumours spread that he wanted to be king.

Suetonius, writing about 150 years later.

Plutarch writing 150 years later.

Caesar forgave those who fought against him.

Cassius Dio, writing 270 years later.

He intends to move the Roman capital to Egypt.

*Rumours in Rome
shortly before Caesar's murder.*

He plans to arrest and kill his rivals.

He has put up his own statue amongst those of the old kings of Rome.

INVESTIGATION

You are the investigator!

1. Look at the timeline of Caesar's life. Explain why he would be famous even without his famous death.

2. Look at the evidence and the timeline. Explain why some senators wanted Caesar dead.

■ Describe what senators were and what power they had (look at the **Big Picture**).

■ Explain why this might make them fear a man like Caesar.

■ List the things Caesar did which would have frightened and angered them. Explain why each action would have had this effect on them.

■ What do you think was the main reason for a group of senators killing Caesar?

From the information in the Big Picture, did the senators succeed in stopping one-man-rule?

Did the rights of women improve?

YOUR MISSION: to examine the changing rights of Roman women.

NEW WORDS

EXPOSE: leave a baby out-of-doors so that it will die. This was sometimes done to girl babies.

SOURCE A

In all the 16 years in which her husband governed Egypt she was never once seen in public and she never let someone from the province into her house. She never let anyone ask her for favours and she never asked for any from her husband.

▲ *Describing the wife of C. Galerius in about AD 50.*

SOURCE B

Women have weak minds, they should be ruled by men.

▲ *A Roman law, from about 450 BC.*

SOURCE C

▲ *Women had control over the household. She was the 'materfamilias' the mother of the family and ran the home. This was always the case.*

SOURCE D

Women shall not sit with men in the amphitheatre.
Women shall not watch athletics (where men competed naked).
No women shall come to the games before 11am (before this men competed naked).

▲ *Laws of Augustus reducing women's freedom after 27 BC.*

SOURCE E

Think of a poor husband who has the embarrassment of being at the sale of the property of his wife and seeing her gladiator's armour being sold. Her armour might be that of a Thracian (armed with helmet, small shield, knife) or a Samnite (armed with large shield, helmet with visor, short sword).

▲ *Written about AD 100. Women gladiators were banned in AD 200.*

INVESTIGATION

You are the investigator!

Look carefully at the evidence in this unit.

1. Identify attitudes towards women before the founding of the Empire in 27 BC. Which of these do you think women would have found most restricting?

SOURCE F

If you have a child keep it if it is a boy but **expose** it if it is a girl.

▲ *Letter from a soldier to his wife in 1 BC.*

SOURCE H

▲ *A girl, her mother and grandmother. A painting from a house in Pompeii, AD 79. Better-off women like this could read and write.*

SOURCE J

▲ *Women were allowed to own and work in shops and this increased during the Empire.*

SOURCE K

▲ *These women athletes lived under the early Empire.*

SOURCE G

▲ *Carving of a woman gladiator.*

SOURCE I

By the law of 169 BC women could not inherit a rich estate but a father could give his property to a male friend who promised to give it to the man's daughter. Under the later Empire it was difficult for a guardian to cheat a woman in his care. Under the Empire the law was relaxed and a daughter could certainly inherit her father's estate.

▲ *From Life and Leisure in Ancient Rome, J. Balsdon, 1969.*

INVESTIGATION

You are the investigator!

2. Make a list of ways freedom for women increased under the Empire.

3. Now make a list of the ways freedom for women decreased under the Empire.

'The rights of women improve over time.' Say what you think, using the evidence. *Remember* your answer may be different in some areas of life compared with others.

THIS CHAPTER ASKS

What was the Roman attitude towards religion?
Which were the main Roman gods?
How did religious ideas change over time?
How and why did Christianity triumph?

Within the Roman Empire people believed in many gods and goddesses. Some of these were the official gods of the Romans themselves. They expected people across the Empire to worship them. But the Romans also respected the gods of other people. They often added them to the list of gods they worshipped. If another tribe's god seemed similar to that of a Roman one the two would be worshipped together. In this way, at the hot springs at what is now Bath, the Romans worshipped the local goddess Sulis and their own goddess Minerva. They also believed that spirits lived in wild places. These they called the 'spirit of the place'. Also, when Emperors died it was believed they became gods.

A CONTRACT NOT A RELATIONSHIP

For Romans their religion did not offer a relationship. It offered a deal to be made. They believed that if they made certain **sacrifices** then the gods would do things for them. This kind of worship was usually done alone or in a small group, not as part of a community of believers. This left many people looking for something more. By about AD 200 new religious beliefs were spreading from the Middle East. The worship of Mithras started in Persia. The worship of Jesus Christ started in Palestine.

SOURCE A

▲ *An altar set up on a bridge in what is now Newcastle. It was set up, as many altars in Northern England, by members of the army. In this case members of the VI Legion.*

Q 1. Imagine you are conducting an interview with a Roman about religion in about AD 200. What answers might she give to your questions:

■ Do you believe in one God or many gods?

■ Why do you try to encourage people in the Empire to worship Roman gods?

■ What is your attitude towards the gods of conquered people?

■ What part do temples and altars play in your worship?

■ Do you believe you have a relationship with your gods?

■ What new religions are spreading across the Empire?

The person who had the job of carrying out a Roman sacrifice was called a 'haruspex'. The word literally means 'gut-gazer'. It was thought that by examining bits of the dead animal's insides the haruspex could foretell the future.

SOME OF THE GODS OF ROME

Jupiter
Called 'greatest and best' by the Romans, Jupiter was the chief Roman god. He was particularly worshipped in the army on their parade grounds. Army altars were sometimes dedicated to Jupiter and the god-Emperor.

Neptune
The god of the sea, he was sometimes pictured riding a sea horse through the waves. His worship was particularly popular with sailors.

Mercury
He was believed to be the messenger of the gods and was also thought to take a particular interest in trade and in bringing in the harvest.

Mars
He was god of war and the month March takes its name from Mars. Sometimes across the Empire also thought to be involved in healing.

Venus
The goddess of love. Oddly enough the chief sewer of Rome was also dedicated to her as goddess of love and the sewer.

Ceres
The goddess of farming. Our modern word 'cereal' comes from the name Ceres. She was also thought to be goddess of laws.

Diana
The goddess of hunting and of wild animals. Diana was also sometimes associated with giving birth.

PLACES OF WORSHIP
The main evidence for Roman worship comes from the remains of temples and stone altars.

TEMPLES
When the tribespeople of thc Iceni led by Boudicca attacked Camulodunum (Colchester) in AD 60 one of the places they destroyed was the great Temple of Claudius. It was a temple where the people of Roman Britain were encouraged to worship the dead Emperor as a god. There were many great temples across the Roman Empire. The Temple of the god-Emperor Augustus at Vienne in Southern Gaul (modern Southern France) was built like that at Colchester to get newly conquered people to join in with worshipping the Emperor.

Others, such as the Temple of Jupiter, Juno (his wife) and Minerva at Dougga in Tunisia, or the Temple of Jupiter at Doliche in modern Turkey, were designed to spread official Roman religion as a way of uniting the Empire.

But most temples were small. They contained a statue of a god or goddess and only the priests went inside. Worshippers made their sacrifices outside and then left. Sometimes animals were killed, or pots, brooches and coins were buried or thrown into springs.

PRIVATE ALTARS
When Antonius Lucretianus paid for a stone altar to be set up, 'To the Italian, German, Gallic and British mother goddesses' at Winchester in Hampshire, he wanted people who saw the altar to know about it afterwards, but he was doing something quite private at the time. This was how most Romans worshipped their gods, whether it was at home or in the countryside.

Most homes contained a small space, or room, called a *lararium*. In this was placed altars, statues of gods and sometimes carvings of dead ancestors. The leading of this family worship was usually done by the father of the family (the *paterfamilias*).

Why did Christianity triumph?

THE BEGINNINGS OF CHRISTIANITY

Around the year AD 30 a poor Jewish teacher named Jesus was crucified by Roman soldiers in what is now Israel. For three years he had been telling people new ideas about the love of God. Some of the leaders of his own people had feared him and persuaded the Roman governor, Pontius Pilate, to execute him.

Within days his followers were telling others that Jesus had risen from the dead. These early friends of Jesus became known as Christians. This name was from a Greek version of the Hebrew word 'messiah', which means a person sent by God. Christians believe that Jesus is God's Son – the Messiah Jesus Christ.

Christians travelled and told others about Jesus. By AD 50 there were Christians in Rome. These communities of Christians became known as the 'Church'.

WHY WERE CHRISTIANS PERSECUTED?

Christians soon found themselves in trouble. They believed in one God. They refused to worship the gods of Rome and the Emperor. This was a crime against the state. Christians were accused of being **atheists** because they said all other gods were not real. This made them unpopular with some people. This made it easy to blame them for things they had not done. Emperor Nero blamed Christians for a great fire in Rome in AD 64. Christians were tortured and killed. One of those killed was the Christian leader, Peter. Another one was Paul who wrote many of the letters in the New Testament.

The persecutions did not happen continually. Some Emperors, such as Domitian (AD 81–96), attacked Christians. Others, such as Trajan (AD 98–117), ignored them. In AD 250 Emperor Decius issued a law requiring all citizens to worship the gods of Rome. When Christians refused they were tortured and killed. By this time many important people had become Christians and **pagans** such as Decius feared they were a threat to the old Roman way of life and ruling. More persecutions followed in AD 303 but in AD 313 the new Emperor, Constantine, made Christianity the official religion of Rome. He believed Christ had helped him win the Battle of the Milvian Bridge, in AD 312, which had made him Emperor.

The Emperor Julian (AD 360–363) tried to turn the Empire back to the old gods of Rome but failed and Christianity continued to grow. Christian leaders became important. In AD 390 the Church leader Bishop Ambrose forced the Emperor Theodosius to say he was sorry for a massacre that had happened in Greece. People listened because more and more of them believed that God was on the side of the Christians. As the Empire declined it was the Christian Church which held many communities together, giving leadership, education and a faith to hold onto.

NEW WORDS

ATHEISTS: people who have no religious belief.
PAGANS: people believing in many gods.
RITES: ways of worship.

SOURCE A

▲ Anti-Christian graffiti from a Roman wall. It shows a donkey crucified.

SOURCE B

Hundreds were arrested more for their anti-social beliefs than for causing fires. They were torn to death by dogs, crucified, or set on fire. As a result people began to feel sorry for them.

▲ Nero's persecutions, described by the Roman Tacitus, AD 118.

SOURCE C

The temples had been almost deserted, religious **rites** long neglected. Until now few purchasers could be found for animals to sacrifice.

▲ The Roman, Pliny, on effects of Christians on Roman religion in Turkey, AD 111–13.

SOURCE D

They wrote in the Greek languages used by many.
Roman peace and roads made it easier to travel.
Many people felt the old religions did not give them
security and moral teaching.
The Christian message was for all.

▲ *Why Christianity spread. Based on* History of Christianity,
1990.

In Rome today you can still visit the tomb of Peter under the Church of St Peter and that of Paul under the Church of St Paul beyond the Wall.

SOURCE E

There was a man named Demetrius who made things
out of silver. He made silver models of the temple of
the goddess Artemis. He brought in a lot of business
for the other skilled workers. One day he called them
together. 'Men', he said. 'You have seen and heard
what this fellow Paul is doing. He says that the gods
we make are not gods at all. Our work is in danger of
losing its good name. People's faith in the temple of
the great goddess Artemis will be weakened.'

▲ *Reactions to the Christian Paul recorded in the New
Testament*

SOURCE F

▲ *A modern painting of the crucifixion of Peter. He died upside down because he thought he was unworthy to die the same way Jesus had.*

Q

1. Look carefully at the evidence. Why were the
early Christians persecuted by the Romans? Think
about:

■ How their beliefs differed from Roman beliefs.

■ The Roman worship of Emperors as gods.

■ How many people's lives were affected by a
challenge to the old Roman beliefs.

■ Explain how this led to persecution.

2. Why did Christianity triumph? Think about:

■ Christian use of the Greek language.

■ Ways of spreading the new ideas.

■ How many people felt about old beliefs.

■ The impact of persecution on ideas about
Christians.

■ The impact of Constantine.

The modern English town of St Albans is named after the first recorded British Christian to be killed by the Roman government for being a Christian. Two others – Julius and Aaron – were killed at Caerleon in Wales.

6 THE END OF THE EMPIRE

1. *AD 117. The most powerful point in the Roman Empire.*

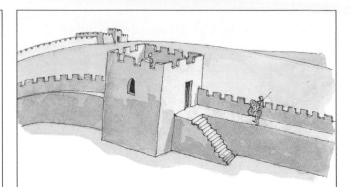

2. *AD 122. Hadrian builds wall to defend British frontier. Other barriers built on German frontier.*

3. *AD 260. Persians capture Emperor Valerian. Revolts across the Empire.*

4. *AD 268-83. Revolts crushed. Persians and Germans defeated.*

5. *Emperors come and go – murdered by their own soldiers.*

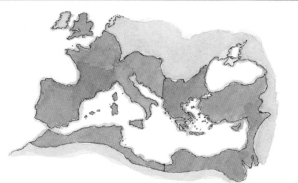

6. *AD 285. Empire split into Western and Eastern parts, each ruled by an Emperor.*

7. *AD 378. Goths revolt and kill Emperor Valens.*

8. *Barbarian tribes raid the Empire – Picts, Scots, Angles and Saxons attack Britain; Franks attack France; desert tribes raid North Africa.*

9. *Plague hits the Empire. Fewer people to pay taxes or fight.*

10. *Trade collapses as the Empire is raided by its enemies.*

11. AD *401 and 407. Goths invade Italy. Capture Rome in* AD *410.*

12. AD *476 Last Emperor, Romulus Augustus, gives up his power. German tribes rule Italy.*

13. *Eastern Roman Empire survives at Constantinople until* AD *1453.*

Q 1. Look at the history cartoon strip. Write the following headings:

■ Weaknesses of the Empire.

■ Enemies of the Empire.

■ Things done to defend the Empire.

■ Victories by enemies of the Empire.

Under each heading make a note of what you can discover. Use your notes to explain the problems faced by the Empire, how it tried to overcome these problems, how and why the Empire collapsed.

In AD 410 the Emperor Honorius wrote to the British cities telling them to defend themselves. Nobody realised it at the time but Britain had just left the Roman Empire. It would never be brought back in.

What have the Romans given us?

In AD 410 the barbarian Goth tribe captured the city of Rome. After this other Roman rulers could not stop the Empire falling apart. In AD 476 the last Roman Emperor, Romulus Augustus, gave up his throne. This was the end of the Roman Empire in the West. What replaced it was a mass of little barbarian kingdoms ruled by Anglo-Saxons, Burgundians, Franks, Goths and Vandals. In the East though the Empire based on Constantinople survived until AD 1453 when it fell to the Turks. But Rome still lives on!

NEW WORDS

ARCHITECTURE: the way a building is designed and built.
CONCRETE: a mixture of gravel, sand, cement and water which sets very hard and strong.
NUMERALS: numbers.

1. Some roads still follow the line of Roman ones.

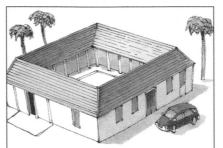
2. Some modern buildings copy Roman architecture.

3. The Christian Church is the largest religion in the world.

4. We still have ideas of a united Europe.

5. Some countries' legal systems copy Roman laws.

6. In the USA they still have a Senate as part of government.

7. Offical names of animals and flowers are in Latin.

8. Latin sayings such as Tempus fugit (time flies)

9. Many schools have a Latin motto.

10. Latin words such as etc, exit.

11. Shakespeare plays on Julius Caesar and Anthony and Cleopatra.

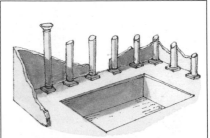
12. Roman ruins still survive to remind us of the past.

13. Cities such as Rome and London were Roman cities.

14. Roman numerals on things like clocks.

15. Clean water and Public Health.

16. Names of months (eg January, August).

17. Names of planets (eg Mars, Jupiter).

18. Latin words on coins.

19. Modern films such as Gladiator.

20. French, Spanish and Italian are based on Latin.

21. Roman inventions such as concrete and the arch.

Q

1. Carry out a survey of your life (at home and in school). Make a list of how the Roman Empire has affected it.

2. Look back on what you have learnt about the Romans.

Why do you think they were so successful? Think about:

■ What they thought about themselves.

■ What they thought about other people.

■ How they organised themselves.

■ Any other things you can think of.

3. Look at all the things that the Romans have done for us. Choose your Top Five. Say why you think these are the most important results of the Roman Empire.

45

Index